☆ ☆ ☆ **1995-1996** ☆ ☆ ☆

HOCKEY SUPERSTARS

Paul Romanuk

Sixteen Super Mini-Posters
of Top Hockey Stars with
Quotes and Facts and
Useful Information plus
Your Own Record Keeper

Scholastic Canada Ltd.
123 Newkirk Road, Richmond Hill, Ontario, Canada

PHOTO CREDITS:

Jason Arnott, Phil Housley © 1995 R. Widner, Protography; Ed Belfour, Keith Tkachuk © 1995 C. Andersen, Bruce Bennett Studios; Raymond Bourque, Chris Chelios © 1995 J. Turner, Protography; Pavel Bure © 1995 A. Foxall, Bruce Bennett Studios; Sergei Fedorov © 1995 B. Miller, Bruce Bennett Studios; Dominik Hasek © 1995 R. Lewis, Bruce Bennett Studios; Jaromir Jagr © 1995 D. Lyons, Photography; Paul Kariya © 1995 R. Rooks, Photography; Trevor Kidd © 1995 M. Hicks, Bruce Bennett Studios; Eric Lindros © 1995 J. McIsaac, Bruce Bennett Studios; Mark Messier (cover), Mark Recchi © 1995 J. Giamundo, Bruce Bennett Studios; Cam Neely © 1995 S. Babineau, Photography; Mats Sundin © 1995 R. Skeoch, Bruce Bennett Studios.

Cover photo of Paul Romanuk © 1995 D. Street, courtesy TSN.

ISBN 0-590-24625-9

5 4 3 2 1   Printed in Canada   5 6 7 8/9

Your Favorite Team — fill this part in at the beginning of the season.

Name of your favorite team: _____

Conference: _____

Division: _____

Players on your favorite team at the start of the season

Number	Name	Position
_____	_____	_____
_____	_____	_____
_____	_____	_____
_____	_____	_____
_____	_____	_____
_____	_____	_____
_____	_____	_____
_____	_____	_____
_____	_____	_____
_____	_____	_____
_____	_____	_____
_____	_____	_____
_____	_____	_____
_____	_____	_____
_____	_____	_____
_____	_____	_____
_____	_____	_____
_____	_____	_____
_____	_____	_____

Changes, Trades, New Players

Fill this section in any time during the season. Use this space to write the names of players who join your team after the start of the season:

_____

_____

_____

_____

I. The Team Standings

Circle the team you think will finish in first place in each of the four NHL Divisions.*

Western Conference

Pacific Division	Central Division
Anaheim Mighty Ducks	Chicago Blackhawks
Calgary Flames	Dallas Stars
Edmonton Oilers	Detroit Red Wings
Los Angeles Kings	St. Louis Blues
San Jose Sharks	Toronto Maple Leafs
Vancouver Canucks	Winnipeg Jets

Eastern Conference

Atlantic Division	Northeast Division
Florida Panthers	Boston Bruins
New Jersey Devils	Buffalo Sabres
New York Islanders	Hartford Whalers
New York Rangers	Montreal Canadiens
Philadelphia Flyers	Ottawa Senators
Tampa Bay Lightning	Pittsburgh Penguins
Washington Capitals	Quebec Nordiques

*At the time of printing, this is how the divisions were arranged. But changes were being predicted — check your newspaper for the correct order.

II. The Playoffs
Which two teams will meet in the Stanley Cup Final?

Western Conference Winner: Eastern Conference Winner:

_____   _____

III. Stanley Cup Final
Which team will win the Stanley Cup?

_____

Your Team — All Season Long

You can keep track of your team's record all season.

The standings of hockey teams are listed on the sports page of the newspaper all season long. The standings will show you which team is in first place, second place, etc., right down to last place.

Some of the abbreviations you will become familiar with are: GP for games played; W for wins; L for losses; T for ties; PTS for points; A for assists; G for goals.

Check the standings on the same day of every month and copy down what they say about your team. By keeping track of your team in this manner you will be able to see when it was playing well and when it wasn't.

Your team: _____ month by month

(put the name of your team here)

DATE	GP	W	L	T	PTS
NOVEMBER 1					
DECEMBER 1					
JANUARY 1					
FEBRUARY 1					
MARCH 1					

Final Standings

At the end of the season print the final record of your team below:

Your Team	GP	W	L	T	PTS

Your Favorite Players' Scoring Records

While you're keeping track of your favorite team during the season, you can also follow the progress of your favorite players. Just fill in their point totals at the start of each month. The abbreviation for points is PTS.

PLAYER	NOVEMBER 1	DECEMBER 1	JANUARY 1	FEBRUARY 1	MARCH 1

Your Favorite Goaltenders' Records

You can keep track of your favorite goaltenders' averages during the season. Just fill in the information below.

GAA is the abbreviation for Goals-Against Average. That is the average number of goals given up by a goaltender during a game over the course of the season.

GOALTENDER	NOVEMBER 1	DECEMBER 1	JANUARY 1	FEBRUARY 1	MARCH 1

Leading Scorers and Goaltenders

At the end of the season you can get the final statistics for your favorite players and the rest of the league.

Fill in the leading scorer and the leading goaltender after the season is over.

NHL Leading Scorer	GP	G	A	PTS

NHL Leading Goaltender	GP	W	L	T	SO	GAA

Your All-Star Picks

Every year at the end of the hockey season, the Professional Hockey Writers Association selects the NHL's First and Second All-Star Teams. Here's a chance for you to make your selections. Remember to pick a player for every position.

First Team

Goaltender: _____

Left Defence: _____

Right Defence: _____

Center: _____

Left Wing: _____

Right Wing: _____

Second Team

Goaltender: _____

Left Defence: _____

Right Defence: _____

Center: _____

Left Wing: _____

Right Wing: _____

The list of the winners will be printed in the newspaper at the end of the season. Tape the list here. How many of your picks are on the team?

The All-Star Game

About halfway through the season there is an All-Star game played in one NHL city. The game features the All-Stars from the Western Conference against the All-Stars from the Eastern Conference.

   Fill this in right after you watch the game on television.

Date of game: _____   Where was it played? _____

Winning team: _____

Final score: _____

The winning goal was scored by: _____

Most valuable player of the game (MVP): _____

Highlights of the Game

The following players scored:

_____   _____

_____   _____

_____   _____

_____   _____

The best play of the game was when: _____

_____

The best save was when: _____

_____

Other highlights: _____

_____

_____

_____

_____

JASON ARNOTT
EDMONTON OILERS

Although the Edmonton Oilers have not been the most successful team in the league for the last couple of seasons, general manager Glen Sather has been laying the groundwork for its sound future by acquiring some of the best young players in the NHL. Of the many quality players in the Oilers lineup working to lift the club back to greatness, the teammate with the heaviest load on his shoulders is Jason Arnott.

Jason was drafted seventh overall by the Oilers in the first round of the 1993 NHL Entry Draft. It was expected that he would return to junior hockey for his final year of eligibility, but he was so impressive at his first Edmonton training camp that he earned a spot on the team at age 19. Jason went on to take a run at the Edmonton rookie scoring record, getting 33 goals and 35 assists for 68 points — just 7 points shy of Jari Kurri's record. Jason ended up finishing second to New Jersey goaltender Martin Brodeur in the vote for NHL Rookie of the Year.

"My rookie year was just a great experience," says Jason. "[You never forget] your first goal, going into some of the great buildings for the first time. It's really special the first time around."

Jason followed up his rookie season by playing on Canada's National Team at the World Championships in Milan, Italy. Canada won a gold medal at that tournament for the first time in 33 years.

"It was the greatest thing I'd ever participated in," says Jason. "I'd never won a gold medal, I'd never represented my country. It will always be something I'll look back at as one of the highlights of my career. I hope to add a Stanley Cup to that one day."

Aside from his part in the Oilers' future plans, Jason is also aware of his role as a hero to many of the young fans who cheer him on.

"I can remember going and asking for an autograph," recalls Jason, "and when you got turned down it was like you took it personally . . . I'd never cheer for that player ever again. When kids come and ask me I try to remember what it was like for me when I was a kid. It's nice that they look up to you."

STATS
Jason Arnott
Edmonton's 1st pick (7th overall) **1993 NHL Entry Draft**
First NHL Team & Season —
Edmonton Oilers 1993–94
Born — **October 11, 1974, in Collingwood, Ontario**
Position — **Center**
Shoots — **Right**
Height — **1.92 m (6'3")**
Weight — **88 kg (195 lbs.)**

Ed
BELFOUR

Goal
CHICAGO BLACKHAWKS

ED BELFOUR
CHICAGO BLACKHAWKS

Considering the amount of hard work he takes on, and his solid performance, Ed Belfour is about as amazing as they come in the NHL these days. Since entering the NHL on a full-time basis in 1990–91, Ed has played in over 80 percent of his team's games and has consistently ranked near or at the top of the league in shutouts and goals-against average.

"Like most top goalies, Eddie is at his best when he plays a lot, and he wants to play a lot," says Chicago coach Darryl Sutter.

The high-water mark in Ed's career so far came in 1990–91, his first full season in the NHL, when he played in 74 of Chicago's 80 games. He led the league with 43 wins and a stellar 2.47 GAA. After that season Ed's home must have looked like a trophy shop! Ed was awarded the Calder Trophy (Rookie of the Year), the Vezina Trophy (Goaltender of the Year), the Jennings Trophy (lowest GAA), plus spots on the NHL All-Rookie and First All-Star Teams.

"There's no question that Ed is in the same category as someone like Patrick Roy," says Chicago's Jeremy Roenick. "There are nights when he will win a game for you. That's what the great ones do."

Last year Ed played behind a Chicago team that was generating more offensive force than in previous years. In particular, the team's power play showed great improvement.

"Sure, it takes a little of the pressure off," says Ed. "When the team is scoring more it gives me a little more margin for error. But I don't think of it in those terms, like I can let in more goals because the team is going to score more. I still want to stop everything. That's the way it has to be for a goalie. As soon as you start thinking any other way you're hurting yourself and the team."

The Blackhawks are hoping that their offensive abilities will remain on the upswing this season. The return of superstar Jeremy Roenick, sidelined late last season with a knee injury, should spark the Hawks once more. And while Roenick drives the team up front, Ed will once again be the backbone of the team — the last line of defence.

STATS
Ed Belfour
Signed as a free agent by Chicago, September 1987
First NHL Team & Season —
Chicago Blackhawks 1988–89
Born — **April 21, 1965, in Carman, Manitoba**
Position — **Goal**
Catches — **Left**
Height — **1.82 m (5'11")**
Weight — **82 kg (182 lbs.)**

Ray
BOURQUE

Defence
BOSTON BRUINS

RAY BOURQUE
BOSTON BRUINS

He's done it all . . . almost. Ray Bourque is one of the greatest defencemen in the history of the NHL. He is a five-time winner of the Norris Trophy and was NHL Rookie of the Year back in 1980. But the award missing from the list, the one that still ignites Ray Bourque, is the big one: the Stanley Cup.

"I want a championship for this franchise," says Ray. "I want to be a part of it and I intend on making it happen. It is the biggest motivator for me at this stage of my career."

Ray and fellow veteran NHL defenceman Paul Coffey are astonishing individuals. They continue not only to play well, but to set the standard of excellence for defencemen. Ray is 35 years old and does not seem at all affected by the passage of time. He is in great shape.

"I have high expectations for myself," says Ray. "I work hard to stay on top of my game. Its not like I'm sitting around looking in the mirror waiting for time to slow me down or make me feel old. Staying in shape is part of the job."

Ray may be one of the toughest defencemen in the NHL, but he knows the difference between being tough and playing dirty. He has never taken 100 penalty minutes in a season. In fact, only once in the last seven seasons has he even surpassed 60 penalty minutes.

"Ray doesn't need to be dirty," says Detroit coach Scott Bowman. "Ray can handle the small speedy players because he has great agility; he can handle the bigger, more physical players because he's so strong."

So how does Ray stack up against the all-time great defencemen? There are those who would place him at number one — the best ever. Ray has dominated his sport for a long time. He has been an All-Star in every season of his 16-year career.

"I've been to the Stanley Cup final twice with the Bruins and that's what it's all about," says Ray. "All of the individual recognition is great, but getting to the final is a thrill. Winning it all would be the biggest thing I could ever do in hockey."

STATS
Ray Bourque
Boston's 1st pick (8th overall)
1979 NHL Entry Draft
First NHL Team & Season —
Boston Bruins 1979–80
Born — **December 28, 1960, in Montreal, Quebec**
Position — **Defence**
Shoots — **Left**
Height — **1.82 m (5′11″)**
Weight — **97.5 kg (215 lbs.)**

Pavel
BURE

Right Wing
VANCOUVER CANUCKS

PAVEL BURE
VANCOUVER CANUCKS

This will be a big year for Pavel Bure. It will give him the chance to prove himself worthy of his 25-million-dollar contract with the Canucks, signed before the start of last season. Although Pavel's playing last year fell short of the mark, he's still a popular draw for the team.

"There are marquee individuals who are the key to your success, and you have to make sure they are on your roster and people can count on coming to see them play for a long time. You're either in business to entertain and win or you're not," says Vancouver co-owner Arthur Griffiths.

One of the most exciting aspects of Pavel's game is his speed. He is one of a handful of players in the game who can lift the fans out of their seats in anticipation of what might happen when he starts to fly down his wing.

"The first time I saw him play, that was what hit me," recalls Vancouver scout Mike Penny. "He was captivating . . . He didn't have much size, but you knew that what he lacked in size was compensated for by his great speed."

Pavel also shows remarkable control around the net; over the course of his first three seasons in the NHL he scored 154 goals. The only other players in NHL history to have done better are Wayne Gretzky and Mike Bossy, two of the greatest goal-scorers of all time.

But Pavel struggled at times last season. He went through one stretch of nine consecutive games without scoring. That was the longest scoring drought of his career.

"It is a tough time for me," said Pavel at the time. "When I can't score I wonder what is wrong with my game. But you just have to keep going back out and doing things that you have done before. I have confidence that I will come back."

To put things in perspective, Pavel in his "off" season still led the team in scoring with 43 points. A tough year for Pavel could be a career year for many of his teammates. Perhaps with the season starting in the fall this year, rather than in January, the "Russian Rocket" — and the Canucks' prospects — will be reignited.

STATS
Pavel Bure
Vancouver's 4th pick (113th overall) 1989 NHL Entry Draft
First NHL Team & Season —
Vancouver Canucks 1991–92
Born — **March 31, 1971, in Moscow, Russia**
Position — **Right Wing**
Shoots — **Left**
Height — **1.80 m (5′10″)**
Weight — **85 kg (189 lbs.)**

CHRIS CHELIOS
CHICAGO BLACKHAWKS

Chris Chelios would be the first to admit that at times during his career he has taken a bad penalty or two. His style is aggressive; he needs to play that way in order to be an effective defenceman in the NHL.

"The thing that makes Chris a great player," says L.A. forward Rick Tocchet, "is that he makes guys think twice about going into the corners or in front of the net with him. He'll give you an extra little jab."

Unfortunately for Chris, sometimes that extra little jab ends up costing the team a penalty. Last season Chris made a determined effort to take fewer penalties while continuing to play his usual tough and aggressive game.

"I wanted to prove to people that I could go out and just play the game and be successful," says Chris. "The thing that has been held against me in the past is that I take bad penalties. I wanted to change people's opinions."

Chris was true to his word: his penalty minute totals were down drastically last season. Chris finished up the year with 72 penalty minutes — an average of less than one minor penalty per game. Chris had topped the 200 penalty minutes total in each of the three previous seasons; in 1992–93 he hit a career high of 282 penalty minutes! Of course, in that same season Chris also won the Norris Trophy as the NHL's best defenceman. Despite his penalties, he played a great season.

"He's still playing his game . . . the same game," says St. Louis forward Brett Hull. "The big thing for Chelly is that he's playing the game between the whistles now. There isn't as much yapping and stuff after the play has stopped. He's still a pain

to play against, just a more controlled pain."

"Chris is at the stage of his career where he's learned a few things," says Chicago coach Darryl Sutter. "He realizes that as one of the leaders of the team he has to set an example. You don't set an example by taking bad penalties. You set an example by playing your game and staying on the ice. He did that for us."

STATS
Chris Chelios
Montreal's 5th pick (40th overall) **1981 NHL Entry Draft**
First NHL Team & Season — **Montreal Canadiens 1983–84**
Born — **January 25, 1962, in Chicago, Illinois**
Position — **Defence**
Shoots — **Right**
Height — **1.85 m (6′1″)**
Weight — **88 kg (186 lbs.)**

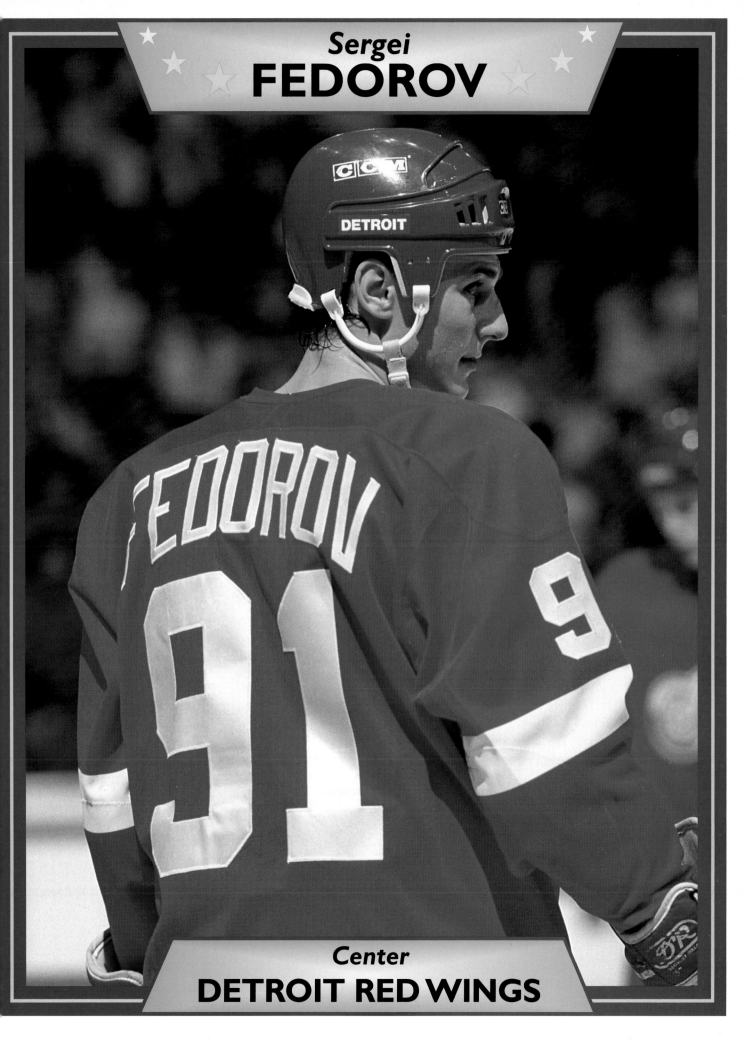

Sergei
FEDOROV

Center
DETROIT RED WINGS

SERGEI FEDOROV
DETROIT RED WINGS

Sergei Fedorov is one of the best two-way forwards in the NHL. He is as effective at his own end of the rink — checking his man or making a good defensive play — as he is at the opponent's end, setting up or finishing off a good scoring chance.

Sergei brings a huge amount of natural talent to the ice; that talent has been further developed under two of the greatest coaches ever. Sergei now plays for Scott Bowman in Detroit, but before he came to North America he played for Victor Tikhonov with the famed Moscow Central Red Army team.

"All I can say about both coaches is that they both know exactly what they want and they both know exactly how to get what they want," says Sergei. "I have learned a lot from both of them."

Sergei has only been playing in the NHL for five seasons. He really came into his own in 1993–94 when he was awarded the Hart Trophy for Most Valuable Player and the Selke Trophy as the league's best defensive forward. The night Sergei was presented with the awards is one he will never forget. The ceremony took place in a jam-packed theater and was being broadcast live on television across Canada.

"It was amazing," he recalls. "There I was with all of those people looking at me and I was trying to think of something to say to everyone. I was so excited and happy . . . I couldn't think of any words that could describe how happy I was."

People in the hockey world have no shortage of words for describing his spectacular abilities on the ice, night after night.

"He reminds me in some ways of Bryan Trottier," says Detroit vice president Jimmy Devellano. "And I should know, because I drafted Trottier back in 1974 when I was with the Islanders."

It's a good comparison: both are great examples of the two-way hockey player. One of the most impressive aspects of Trottier's career, and something Sergei aspires to, is the ability to enjoy success over the long haul. Time will be the ultimate judge, but so far Sergei is right on the mark.

STATS
Sergei Fedorov
Detroit's 4th pick (74th overall)
1989 NHL Entry Draft
First NHL Team & Season —
Detroit Red Wings 1990–91
Born — **December 13, 1969, in Pskov, Russia**
Position — **Center**
Shoots — **Left**
Height — **1.85 (6'1")**
Weight — **90 kg (200 lbs.)**

Dominik
HASEK

Goal
BUFFALO SABRES

DOMINIK HASEK
BUFFALO SABRES

Just call him "The Dominator."

For the last two seasons, there has been no better goalie in the NHL than Dominik Hasek. Two years ago, Dominik became the first NHL goalie in 20 years to finish the regular season with a goals-against average below 2.00. His numbers in 93–94 were impressive: 30 wins, 20 losses and 6 ties with a 1.95 GAA. At the end of it all, he was voted the best goaltender in the league and named to the NHL's First All-Star Team.

It is hard to imagine that as recently as the 1991–92 season Dominik was toiling away in the Chicago Blackhawks minor league system, on the heels of a career as one of the finest goaltenders in Europe. He held little hope of ever being Chicago's number-one goaltender. But his NHL career turned around in Buffalo.

As last year got underway there was little question that Dominik would be number one with the Sabres again. But after the NHL lockout, Dominik got off to a slow start. It was suggested by some that he wasn't in game shape.

"I wasn't in the best shape when I headed to training camp," says Dominik. "I came in from the Czech Republic and felt tired and not very comfortable. I came around after a few games."

But then Dominik went down with a rotator-cuff injury. It was feared at one stage that the injury could be serious and might even require surgery.

"I didn't feel good," says Dominik. "It hurt to lift and move my arm. I was happy that I wasn't out for as long as some people thought I would be."

Dominik came back and seemed rejuvenated. By the second half of the season he was once again the dominant goaltender he had been the season before.

"Dominik doesn't play the most orthodox style," says coach John Muckler, "but in the last couple of seasons I can't think of a goalie who has been more effective. Most times when we need the big save in a close game we can count on him. He frustrates shooters because he doesn't always look as though he's in position, then he robs you."

"One of the most impressive things about Dominik is that he just doesn't give up," says Boston forward Cam Neely. "He'll look like he's out of it and then, all of a sudden, he's not. He'll stretch, fire out his leg, whatever . . . he doesn't give up on it."

STATS
Dominik Hasek
Chicago's 11th pick (199th overall) **1983 NHL Entry Draft**
First NHL Team & Season —
Chicago Blackhawks 1990–91
Born — **January 29, 1965, in Pardubice, Czech Republic**
Position — **Goal**
Catches — **Left**
Height — **1.82 m (5'11")**
Weight — **74.5 kg (165 lbs.)**

Phil
HOUSLEY

Defence
CALGARY FLAMES

PHIL HOUSLEY
CALGARY FLAMES

For a while it looked as though Phil Housley would spend his entire career with the Buffalo Sabres. Phil was drafted sixth overall by the Sabres in the first round of the 1982 NHL Entry Draft, and he spent the next eight seasons with that club. But over the last five seasons Phil has been shuttled from the Winnipeg Jets to the St. Louis Blues and, finally, to the Calgary Flames.

"Being traded is part of the game," Phil has said on several occasions.

Even if being traded is part of the game, it always raises questions about the real reason behind it. With every trade comes speculation.

"A team trading for Housley is looking for a good offensive defenceman," says one NHL scout. "But the reason he may be traded away is that some people think his defence can be a little suspect . . . [still,] most teams in this league would love to have a defenceman with the offensive skills he has."

The Flames acquired Phil from St. Louis before the start of last season as part of a deal that sent Al MacInnis to the Blues. Phil went on to become part of Calgary's gifted defensive corps, with Zarley Zalapski, James Patrick and Steve Chiasson.

"One of the biggest things we have going for us is the speed of our defence," says Phil. "With speed we can usually get the puck back in our end and start to move it out before the other team's forecheckers get in on top of us."

Phil looked good last year, after an injury-filled 1993–94 season during which he missed a total of 58 games. A back injury was his most serious, keeping him out of 53 games in a row.

"It was frustrating when it seemed like I was constantly injured," recalls Phil. "Coming back from a back injury is always tough. I had confidence that I was fully recovered but I still wanted to go out and prove to people that there were no problems."

Phil finished off last season with 43 points — tied for second in scoring among defencemen. By all indications it is clear: Phil is back and ready to play at full strength.

STATS
Phil Housley
Buffalo's 1st pick (6th overall)
1982 NHL Entry Draft
First NHL Team & Season —
Buffalo Sabres 1982–83
Born — **March 9, 1964, in St. Paul, Minnesota**
Position — **Defence**
Shoots — **Left**
Height — **1.80 m (5'10")**
Weight — **88 kg (185 lbs.)**

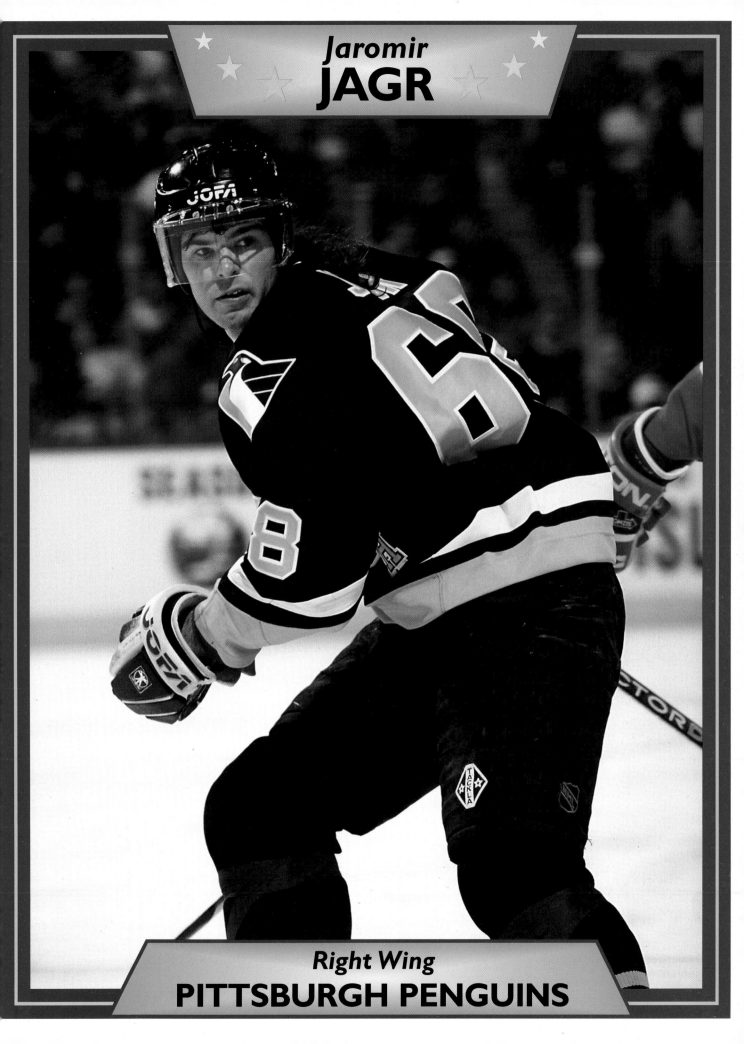

JAROMIR JAGR
PITTSBURGH PENGUINS

As any hockey fan knows, Pittsburgh Penguin Mario Lemieux is one of the greatest players in the history of the game — but only when he is in good health. While Mario has been battling Hodgkin's disease the last couple of seasons, Pittsburgh's number 68, Jaromir Jagr, has been sensational. Jaromir has led the Penguins in scoring for the last two seasons, and continues to cultivate a style of play that is productive for the team and electrifying for the fans.

"He's his own man, that's for sure," says teammate Luc Robitaille. "He has his own way of going about things . . . but he's a winner and a great offensive player for the team."

Along with his great skills, Jaromir exudes a confident attitude that some might call cocky. But Jaromir has every reason to have confidence in his on-ice ability. Between 1992 and 1994 he reeled off back-to-back 90-point seasons. If last season had been the usual 84 games, instead of a short season of 48, Jaromir's stats would have broken through the 90-point barrier for the third time in a row. And many of the goals Jaromir scores are vital ones: he has led the team in game-winning goals in each of the last two seasons.

"We knew when Mario was having health problems that we would be in big trouble if other players on the team weren't able to rise to the occasion, to try to pull up some of the slack," says Pittsburgh general manager Craig Patrick. "He's always been a hungry kid. He has always wanted more."

"Before Mario was injured I never thought much about goals," says Jaromir. "It was success to me just to beat a guy with a good pass. But you have to score to win games. Before, with Mario here, everybody knew he was going to score goals. With him out I know that I have to score more."

"There are only a handful of guys who can get their hands on the puck and make it all happen," says Washington general manager David Poile. "He has great size, strength and outside speed. He's one of the best."

STATS
Jaromir Jagr
Pittsburgh's 1st pick (5th overall) **1990 NHL Entry Draft**
First NHL Team & Season — **Pittsburgh Penguins 1990–91**
Born — **February 15, 1972, in Kladno, Czech Republic**
Position — **Right Wing**
Shoots — **Left**
Height — **1.90 m (6'2")**
Weight — **94 kg (208 lbs.)**

Paul
KARIYA

Left Wing
MIGHTY DUCKS OF ANAHEIM

PAUL KARIYA
MIGHTY DUCKS OF ANAHEIM

Throughout his short amateur and professional career Paul Kariya has displayed a remarkable level of adaptability. Paul has been able to modify and develop his talents to suit the U.S. college game, international hockey and, last year, the NHL.

"Something I've learned during my life," says Paul, "is that you always have to adapt. You have to change to meet the situation, you don't want to become predictable."

One aspect of Paul's career has been predictable: success. He was a prolific scorer with his British Columbia junior team, the Penticton Panthers. In his final season with that team Paul picked up 132 points in 40 games, an average of better than 3 points per game. In his first season with the NCAA Maine Black Bears, Paul was named winner of the Hobey Baker Award as the best player in U.S. college hockey. Paul was the first freshman ever to win the award.

In 1994, before turning pro, Paul turned in some great performances with the Canadian Olympic team and Canada's National Team at the World Hockey Championship. At the Olympics Paul had seven points, helping Canada to win a silver medal; at the World Championship Paul led the team in scoring, with 12 points in eight games, and Canada won its first gold medal at that tournament in 33 years.

"Success at the team level is the greatest thing," says Paul. "I've come to appreciate that in the last couple of years, when I was part of teams that won things. That's the best feeling. All I care about right now is winning the Stanley Cup."

Chances are that the Mighty Ducks have a few years of fine-tuning ahead of them before taking a run at the Cup. Paul still has some adjusting to do, too.

"It's a different game here in the NHL," says Paul's coach Ron Wilson. "We want Paul to continue to be creative when we have the puck. Before he can do that, he has to help the other four guys on the ice get the puck back. That's the biggest change he has to make in his game."

One change Paul won't have to make is his position in the Mighty Ducks' future — it will continue to be front and center.

STATS
Paul Kariya
Anaheim's 1st pick (4th overall)
1993 NHL Entry Draft
First NHL Team & Season —
**Mighty Ducks of Anaheim
1994–95**
Born — **October 16, 1974, in Vancouver, British Columbia**
Position — **Left Wing**
Shoots — **Left**
Height — **1.82 m (5'11")**
Weight — **79 kg (175 lbs.)**

Trevor KIDD

Goal
CALGARY FLAMES

TREVOR KIDD CALGARY FLAMES

Trevor Kidd finally got his chance last season to be a number-one goaltender in the NHL. His journey toward that destination took him from Canada's National Team, to the Olympics, to the International Hockey League and, finally, to the number-one spot with the Calgary Flames. Trevor was drafted eleventh overall by the Flames in the first round of the 1990 NHL Entry Draft. Since 1969, only seven goalies have been drafted in the top 10.

Trevor left junior hockey with excellent credentials. He helped to backstop Canada's National Junior Team to a world championship in 1990; he also led the Spokane Chiefs to a Memorial Cup title in 1991. During the 1991 junior hockey playoffs Trevor lost only one game. His record was 14–1 with a 2.06 GAA.

"The Memorial Cup was a big thrill for me," says Trevor. "There were still people who questioned what kind of a goaltender I could be when things got down to the big games. I had a good Memorial Cup tournament, with a great team."

After junior hockey Trevor joined Canada's National and Olympic teams for the 1991–92 season. He ended up playing one game at the 1992 Olympics, helping Canada to win a silver medal.

"The Olympics was a great thing to be involved in," says Trevor. "Sean Burke was the number-one goalie . . . but just to be a part of the Olympic experience was special. It's something I'll never forget."

Trevor got his shot at the top job in Calgary last season after longtime number-one man Mike Vernon was traded to the Detroit Red Wings.

"It was time for a change, and we felt that Trevor was ready for the number-one spot," said former Calgary coach Dave King at the time. "Trevor is a real competitor and a solid National Hockey League goalie. He's a real asset to our club."

One of the most important advantages any NHL goalie can have is confidence. Trevor's seemed to reach an all-time high last season.

"It's nice to know that the team and the coach has confidence in you," says Trevor. "It helps you to stay sharp when you know that you'll be in there most nights."

Trevor is only 23 years old, and is considered to be one of the best young goalies in the NHL. There is little question that he'll be right in there again for the Calgary Flames this season.

STATS
Trevor Kidd
Calgary's 1st pick (11th overall) **1990 NHL Entry Draft**
First NHL Team & Season —
Calgary Flames 1993–94
Born — **March 29, 1972, in Dugald, Manitoba**
Position — **Goal**
Catches — **Left**
Height — **1.90 m (6′2″)**
Weight — **86 kg (190 lbs.)**

Eric
LINDROS

Center
PHILADELPHIA FLYERS

ERIC LINDROS
PHILADELPHIA FLYERS

Eric Lindros is one of the greatest players in the world — he is doing exactly what the hockey world has expected of him since as far back as 1989. And, for that matter, being a great player is exactly what Eric expects of himself.

"He plays so hard every night," says Flyers coach Terry Murray. "There is no one harder on Eric than Eric. He'll adjust and realize that you can't make a big play every time you're on the ice . . . his game will become more mature. That's progression."

Last year, at age 21, Eric became the tenth captain in Flyers history — and the youngest captain in the NHL. Eric's first year as captain was a learning experience; he expects to continue growing into the job this season.

"You live and learn, take your lumps and find out how to do things the right way and gain the confidence of your teammates," says Eric.

Eric gained the confidence of his teammates long before last year. During his first two years with the team it was obvious to anyone who watched how much better the Flyers had become. The team scored more, had more confidence and won more games with Eric playing for them. But for many it was last season when Eric really pulled his game up to a higher level. Part of what helped Eric was a timely deal pulled off by the Flyers on February 9, 1995. The team obtained John LeClair, Gilbert Dionne and Eric Desjardins from the Montreal Canadiens, in return for Mark Recchi and a 1995 third round draft pick. Eric was put on a line with John and Mikael Renberg and the three clicked immediately.

"A big part of my success is two great linemates," says Eric. "John LeClair, Mikael Renberg and I really communicate well on the ice . . . it's like we know where the other guy is going to be. A lot of what they do allows me to be better."

The line was billed by some as the "Legion of Doom." The nickname was an appropriate one, because the trio often spelled doom for its opponents. With the line in action, the Flyers vaulted to the top of the standings in the Atlantic Division.

Eric may already be a dominant force in the game but, like any perfectionist, he wants to become even better. He believes he can do that by learning more about hockey.

"I look at some players that I'm bigger than and faster than, but they get there because they know the game a little better," says Eric. "I want to understand the game more. I think it can be a real advantage to you. That's the name of the game, isn't it? Having more advantages than your opponent."

STATS
Eric Lindros
Quebec's 1st pick (1st overall)
1991 NHL Entry Draft
First NHL Team & Season —
Philadelphia Flyers 1992–93
Born — **February 28, 1973, in London, Ontario**
Position — **Center**
Shoots — **Right**
Height — **1.95 (6'4")**
Weight — **104 kg (229 lbs.)**

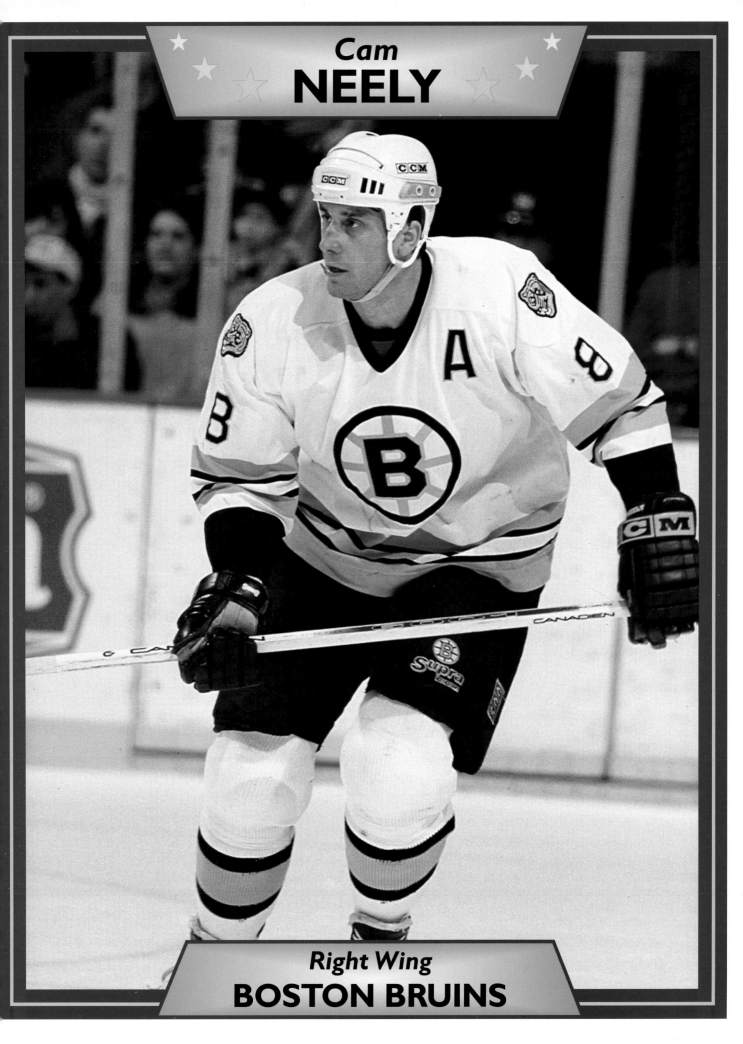

Cam
NEELY

Right Wing
BOSTON BRUINS

CAM NEELY
BOSTON BRUINS

Cam Neely should have been finished as a star hockey player back around 1992. Cam struggled with injuries to his thigh and left knee for the better part of two seasons; from 1991 until the end of the 1993 season he only played in 22 games. But as one of the most persistent players in the NHL, Cam saw the two seasons of frustration as a test of his character and determination — a test he continues to pass with flying colors every time out.

Two seasons ago, Cam rebounded from his two-year nightmare with one of the greatest comeback seasons in NHL history. Cam scored 50 goals in 44 games; he finished up the season with 50 goals and 24 assists for 74 points in 49 games, with 14 multiple-goal games and 3 hat tricks. For his great season Cam was presented with the Bill Masterton Trophy, awarded annually to a player for "perseverance, sportsmanship and dedication to hockey."

"It's nice to get recognition for coming back from something people didn't expect you to come back from," says Cam. "I never lost hope; I worked hard. But the toughest part of the rehab was definitely the mental rehabilitation . . . believing [I] could do it."

If Cam had any doubts, none of his present or former teammates or coaches ever did.

"Cam's greatest asset is his mental toughness," says Boston coach and former teammate Steve Kasper. "Cam is willing to work hard and pay the price. Watch him on the ice: nothing gets in his way. He's a real inspiration."

Cam injured his right knee late in the 1993–94 season, but came back again last season to lead the Bruins in goal scoring.

What continues to fuel him after he has faced so many physical setbacks in his career? No doubt his love of playing the game.

Randy Burridge, a former teammate of Cam's, has also battled knee problems during his career. Randy says inspiration is the key.

"This is such a great game. To pack it in because of an injury, without giving it your best shot to come back, would be shortchanging yourself. I think, ultimately, you'd feel cheated," says Randy. "You have the rest of your life to be retired, but you can only play this game for so long. You might as well enjoy it for as long as you can."

STATS
Cam Neely
Vancouver's 1st pick (9th overall) **1983 NHL Entry Draft**
First NHL Team & Season — **Vancouver Canucks 1983–84**
Born — **June 6, 1965, in Comox, British Columbia**
Position — **Right Wing**
Shoots — **Right**
Height — **1.85 m (6'1")**
Weight — **98 kg (218 lbs.)**

MARK RECCHI
MONTREAL CANADIENS

About halfway through last season it became apparent that the Montreal Canadiens were in desperate need of offensive strength: the team was averaging fewer than three goals per game. It was time for a trade. Within a month Montreal general manager Serge Savard made two of them. He obtained sniper Mark Recchi from the Philadelphia Flyers and, about a month later, picked up Pierre Turgeon from the New York Islanders. It wasn't an easy decision to make: to get Mark, the Canadiens had to give up forwards Gilbert Dionne and John LeClair and defenceman Eric Desjardins. In the deal for Pierre, Montreal lost defenceman Mathieu Schneider and team captain Kirk Muller. But after the second deal, Pierre and Mark were put on an offensive line with Vincent Damphousse, and Montreal finally showed some punch.

"We acquired two players that gave us something we didn't have before," says Montreal general manager Serge Savard.

Mark's game seemed to pick up after Pierre joined the team. But there was a lot of pressure on Mark at the outset, because one of the players he had been exchanged for was excelling with his new team.

"That makes it tough. People see how well John LeClair is playing with the Flyers and they wonder why I'm not doing the same thing here," said Mark. "All I can say is that I know what I can do and I know that I can help this team offensively."

In each of the four years before last, Mark averaged 110 points per season. He started his career with the Pittsburgh Penguins; before being traded to Philadelphia, Mark had a 113-point season with the Penguins and played a big role in the team's Stanley Cup Championship of 1991.

"We have a guy who is a winner," says Montreal coach Jacques Demers. "How often do you get a chance to pick up a 100-point scorer like Mark Recchi? A 100-point scorer who has played on a Stanley Cup champion?"

"I feel good about the trade," says Mark. "Montreal is a great organization and I feel a lot of pride wearing the jersey. It will be nice to start fresh right at the beginning of a season with the team and hopefully be part of things coming together for us."

STATS
Mark Recchi
Pittsburgh's 4th pick (67th overall) 1988 NHL Entry Draft
First NHL Team & Season —
Pittsburgh Penguins 1988–89
Born — **February 1, 1968, in Kamloops, British Columbia**
Position — **Right Wing**
Shoots — **Left**
Height — **1.80 (5'10")**
Weight — **83 kg (185 lbs.)**

Mats
SUNDIN

Center/Right Wing
TORONTO MAPLE LEAFS

MATS SUNDIN
TORONTO MAPLE LEAFS

It was a badly kept secret in the hockey world: the Quebec Nordiques wanted to make a deal that would help the team achieve a big turnaround. Despite having some of the best young talent in the NHL, the Nordiques had never come close to reaching the success most had predicted — and expected.

On June 28, 1994, at the NHL Draft in Hartford, the Nordiques pulled off a deal designed to change the direction and character of the team. The Nordiques obtained Wendel Clark, Sylvain Lefebvre and Landon Wilson from the Toronto Maple Leafs in exchange for Garth Butcher, Todd Warriner and Mats Sundin. For Nordiques general manager Pierre Lacroix, trading Sundin was a tough, but necessary, part of the deal.

"Mats was a number one [draft pick] overall. It's always tough to trade a player of that caliber," says Lacroix. "Mats is a very good NHL player and could be a great player someday . . . but we had to give something up to get something."

There were other factors involved too. For one, Mats didn't feel as though he was being treated as well as some of his teammates in Quebec.

"Mats was unhappy with his situation," says his agent Mark Perrone. "We had been trying to work something out for a few months. The two main options left were making Mats happy where he was and paying him accordingly, or trading him somewhere else."

"Toronto is a great hockey city and [the Maple Leafs] is a great organization," says Mats. "I was excited about coming here as soon as I heard about it."

Mats certainly played like he was excited about coming to Toronto — he was one of the most exciting offensive players in the league last year, and a major part of Toronto's offence. Mats is a big player and is at his best when he is using that size to drive toward the net and create scoring chances. Many felt that Mats was doing more of that last season. He led the team with 23 goals and 47 points.

"It depends on which guys you are playing with," says Mats. "The guys I was with made me feel more confident about driving toward the net. They helped to create some room for me out there."

Mats' best season in the NHL so far has been 1992–93 — when he finished up with 47 goals and 67 assists for 114 points. But there seems to be little doubt that Mats can do much better than that before his career is over. He is only 24 years old, and he has the potential to be one of the best if he puts his mind to it.

STATS
Mats Sundin
Quebec's 1st pick (1st overall)
1989 NHL Entry Draft
First NHL Team & Season —
Quebec Nordiques 1990–91
Born — **February 13, 1971, in Bromma, Sweden**
Position — **Center/Right Wing**
Shoots — **Right**
Height — **1.95 m (6'4")**
Weight — **92 kg (204 lbs.)**

Keith
TKACHUK

Left Wing
WINNIPEG JETS

KEITH TKACHUK
WINNIPEG JETS

Just call him one of the hardest-working and most overlooked players in the NHL. Two years ago Keith was made captain of the Jets; he responded by leading the team in goals (41), assists (40) and points (81), while setting career highs in all three categories. Keith was assigned the captaincy during his second full season with Winnipeg.

"The thing that made Keith a natural choice for captain," says Winnipeg general manager John Paddock, "was the level of respect he receives from his teammates and other players in the league. He is respected because he works hard all the time."

Hard work has always been a big part of Keith's game. He was named to the Hockey East All-Rookie Team back in 1990–91 when he was playing with Boston University. His hard work and determination also earned him a place on the U.S. National Junior Team in 1990–91 and 1991–92. And he helped the US Olympic team to a fourth-place finish at the 1992 Winter Olympic Games in Albertville, France.

Keith is one of the best power forwards in the NHL; he is a strong skater and tough to move off the puck. And he has enough control around the net to take advantage of the offensive opportunities that he creates.

Last season Keith continued as the heart of the Jets. He was a part of one of the most successful lines in the NHL: the "Olympic line," so-called because all three players — Keith, Teemu Selanne and Alexei Zhamnov — had played in the Olympic games. Keith had played for the USA, Teemu for Finland and Alexei for Russia. The three brought a high level of skill and excitement to the games they played together.

"There were times during the season when we weren't playing that well as a team . . . John would try to put the three of us together and play us as much as possible," says Keith.

Occasionally the line would be split up, in order to add more depth to the Winnipeg attack.

"It would have been nice to have played the three of them together all the time," says Paddock, "but there were times when the best thing for the team was to split them up to try and get other lines going."

All three players on the Olympic line finished in the league top 20 in scoring. Keith had 51 points — reinforcing his position as one of the top players in the NHL.

STATS
Keith Tkachuk
Winnipeg's 1st pick (19th overall) **1990 NHL Entry Draft**
First NHL Team & Season — **Winnipeg Jets 1991–92**
Born — **March 28, 1972, in Melrose, Massachusetts**
Position — **Left Wing**
Shoots — **Left**
Height — **1.90 m (6'2")**
Weight — **95 kg (210 lbs.)**

Penalties

Do you know what is happening when the referee stops play and makes a penalty call? If you don't, then you're missing an important part of the game. The referee can call different penalties that result in everything from playing a man short for two minutes to having a player kicked out of the game.

Here are some of the most common referee signals. Now you'll know what penalties are being called against your team.

Boarding
Pounding the closed fist of one hand into the open palm of the other hand.

Charging
Rotating clenched fists around one another in front of the chest.

Cross-checking
A forward and backward motion with both fists clenched extending from the chest.

Elbowing
Tapping the elbow of the "whistle hand" with the opposite hand.

High-sticking
Holding both fists, clenched, one above the other.

Holding
Clasping wrist of the "whistle hand" well in front of the chest.

Hooking
A tugging motion with both arms, as if pulling something toward the stomach.

Roughing
A thrusting motion with the arm extending from the side.

Interference
Crossed arms stationary in front of the chest with fists closed.

Slashing
A chopping motion with the edge of one hand across the opposite forearm.

Tripping
Striking the right leg with the right hand below the knee while keeping both skates on the ice.

Wash-out
Both arms swung laterally across the body with palms facing down. Used by the referee, it means no goal.

Spearing
A jabbing motion with both hands thrust out in front of the body.

Unsportsmanlike conduct
Use both hands to form a "T" in front of the chest.

Your Own Hockey Career

Whether you play in a league, at school, or just for recreation, it's fun to keep track of how you and your team do during the season.

This section is for you to fill in with the details of your hockey career — both the high points and the low points.

Your team's name: _____

Name of the league: _____

Position you play: _____

Your team nickname: _____

Some of the other players on the team:

_____   _____

_____   _____

_____   _____

_____   _____

_____   _____

_____   _____

_____   _____

Season Highlights
The most exciting game you played in this season was: _____

_____

_____

Your own best game was: _____

_____

_____

_____

The best team you played against this season was: _____

_____

The closest game you played was: _____

_____

Your worst game was: _____

_____

_____

The funniest thing that happened to you during a hockey game this season was:

_____

_____

Here's your own personal score sheet — fill this out after every game.

	OTHER TEAM	GOALS	ASSISTS	POINTS
GAME #1				
GAME #2				
GAME #3				
GAME #4				
GAME #5				
GAME #6				
GAME #7				
GAME #8				
GAME #9				
GAME #10				

The Stanley Cup Playoffs

The Stanley Cup Playoffs start in April and usually run until the end of May. Before reaching the final, teams must first win their respective Division and Conference championships.

Keep track below:

Pacific Division Champion: _____

Central Division Champion: _____

Western Conference Champion: _____

Atlantic Division Champion: _____

Northeast Division Champion: _____

Eastern Division Champion: _____

Stanley Cup Final:

Which two teams played? _____

Who won? _____

How many games did the series go to? _____

Who was the Playoff MVP? _____

Clip a picture from the newspaper of the winning team
with the Stanley Cup after the final game. Tape the picture below.

The Final — Game-by-Game

Fill out this part of your record keeper after each game of the
Stanley Cup Final while you can still feel the excitement!
Fill in the final score, where the game was played, who scored
and any other information you can think of.

GAME 1 _____
_____

GAME 2 _____
_____

GAME 3 _____
_____

GAME 4 _____
_____

GAME 5 _____
_____

GAME 6 _____
_____

GAME 7 _____
_____

NHL Awards

Here are some of the major NHL awards for individual players. Fill in your selection for each award and then fill in the name of the actual winner of the trophy.

HART MEMORIAL TROPHY

Awarded to the player judged to be the most valuable to his team. Selected by the Professional Hockey Writers Association.

Your choice: _____ The winner: _____

ART ROSS TROPHY

Awarded to the player who leads the league in scoring points at the end of the regular season.

Your choice: _____ The winner: _____

CALDER MEMORIAL TROPHY

Awarded to the player selected as the most proficient in his first year of competition in the NHL. Selected by the Professional Hockey Writers Association.

Your choice: _____ The winner: _____

JAMES NORRIS TROPHY

Awarded to the defence player who demonstrates throughout his season the greatest all-round ability. Selected by the Professional Hockey Writers Association.

Your choice: _____ The winner: _____

VEZINA TROPHY

Awarded to the goalkeeper judged to be the best. Selected by the NHL general managers.

Your choice: _____ The winner: _____

WILLIAM JENNINGS TROPHY

Awarded to the goalkeepers who have played a minimum of 25 games for the team with the fewest goals scored against it.

Your choice: _____   The winner: _____

LADY BYNG MEMORIAL TROPHY

Awarded to the player judged to have exhibited the best sportsmanship combined with a high standard of playing ability. Selected by the Professional Hockey Writers Association.

Your choice: _____   The winner: _____

FRANK SELKE TROPHY

Awarded to the forward who best excels in the defensive aspects of the game. Selected by the Professional Hockey Writers Association.

Your choice: _____   The winner: _____

CONN SMYTHE TROPHY

Awarded to the player most valuable to his team in the Stanley Cup Playoffs. Selected by the Professional Hockey Writers Association.

Your choice: _____   The winner: _____

BILL MASTERTON MEMORIAL TROPHY

Awarded to the player who best exemplifies the qualities of perseverance, sportsmanship and dedication to hockey. Selected by the Professional Hockey Writers Association.

Your choice: _____   The winner: _____